DONATED BY
AGWUNOBI FAMILY

The Kids' Career Library™

A Day in the Life of a
Doctor

Mary Bowman-Kruhm
and Claudine G. Wirths

The Rosen Publishing Group's
PowerKids Press™
New York

Thanks to Robin Miller, M.D., Wayne Crowder, M.D., Zöe Gibson, and Scott Eargle.

Published in 1997 by The Rosen Publishing Group, Inc.
29 East 21st Street, New York, NY 10010

First Edition

Book Design: Erin McKenna

Photo Illustrations: Cover and all photo illustrations by Kelly Hahn.

Bowman-Kruhm, Mary.
    A day in the life of a doctor/ by Mary Bowman-Kruhm and Claudine G. Wirths.
        p.   cm. — (Kids' career library)
    Includes index.
    Summary: Describes the daily responsibilities and tasks in the life of a doctor.
    ISBN 0-8239-5096-4
    1. Medicine—Vocational guidance—Juvenile literature. 2. Physicians—Juvenile literature. [1. Physicians. 2. Occupations.] I. Wirths, Claudine G. II. Title. III. Series.
R690.B649 1997
610.69'52—dc21
                                                                                        96-53130
                                                                                           CIP
                                                                                            AC

Manufactured in the United States of America

Contents

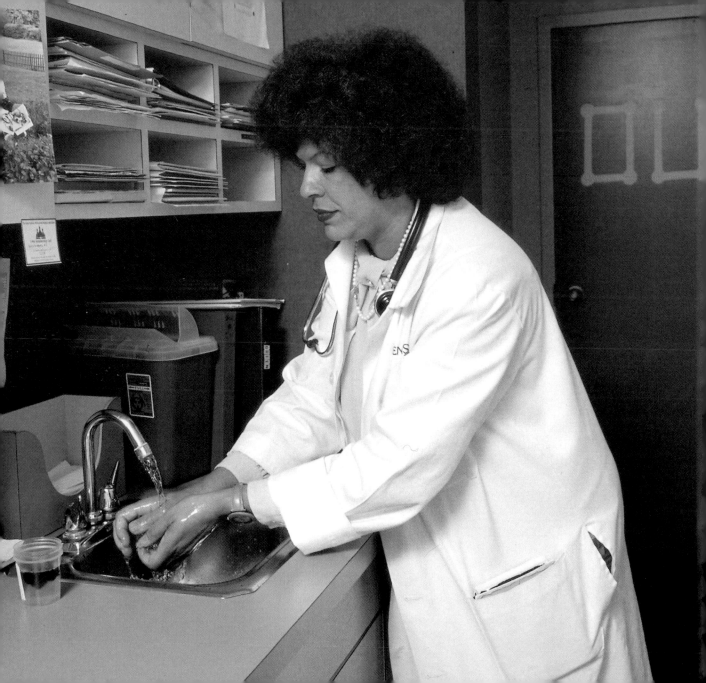

Dr. Miller's Day Begins

When Dr. Robin Miller gets to her office, lots of people who are sick or hurt are waiting to see her. She puts on her white coat and washes her hands with lots of soap and water. She will wash her hands after she sees each **patient** (PAY-shunt) so that **germs** (JERMZ) will not travel from one sick person to another.

Now Dr. Miller is ready to start her day.

◀ Dr. Miller uses a special soap to remove germs from her hands.

Taking a Look

Dr. Miller's first patient is a woman. She sits on the table.

"My ear hurts," the woman says.

"Let me take a look," says Dr. Miller.

Dr. Miller looks in the woman's ear with an **otoscope** (AH-tuh-skohp). The ear is **infected** (in-FEK-ted). Dr. Miller writes that on the woman's chart. She also writes down what medicine the woman will need.

"The medicine will help," says Dr. Miller. "You should feel better soon."

Dr. Miller uses a special tool to look in her patient's ear. ▶

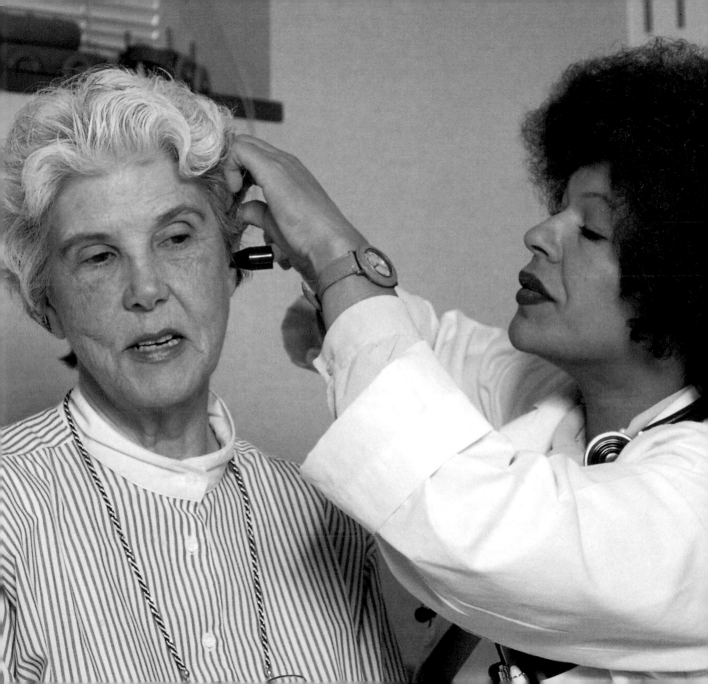

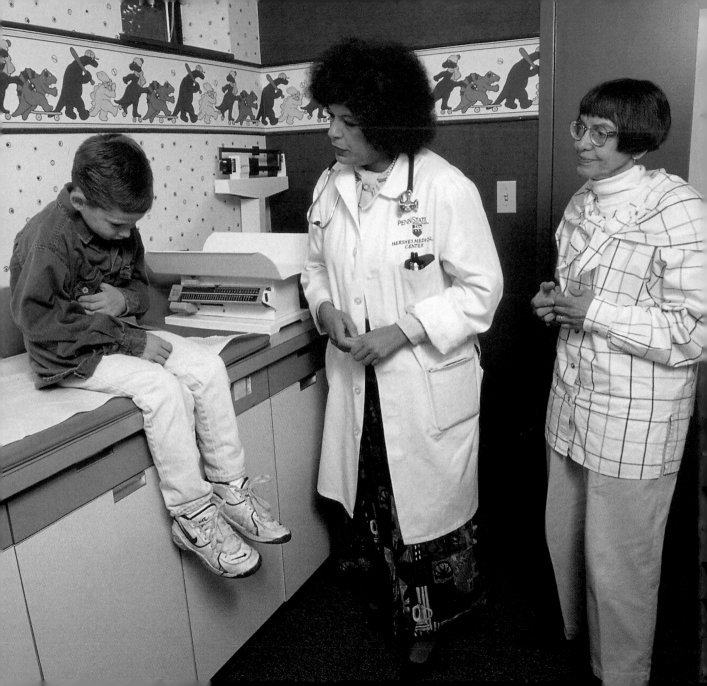

Scott

A boy comes into the room next. His grandmother is with him.

"My name is Scott," says the boy.

"My name is Dr. Miller. How can I help you?"

"I've been sick all week," Scott says.

"He gets tired when he plays," his grandmother adds. "And he doesn't eat very much. I don't know what's wrong. I am worried about him."

◀ Scott and his grandmother explain to Dr. Miller how Scott has been feeling.

9

A Great Patient

Dr. Miller **examines** (egg-ZAM-inz) Scott. She listens to his heart with her **stethoscope** (STETH-uh-skohp). She checks Scott's tummy. She even looks inside his ears and mouth.

"Scott, you have a **virus** (VY-rus)," says Dr. Miller. "You don't need any medicine. But you need to get some rest. You should feel fine in a couple of days. You can hop down from the table now. You were a great patient."

Dr. Miller can hear what is happening inside Scott's chest with a stethoscope. ▶

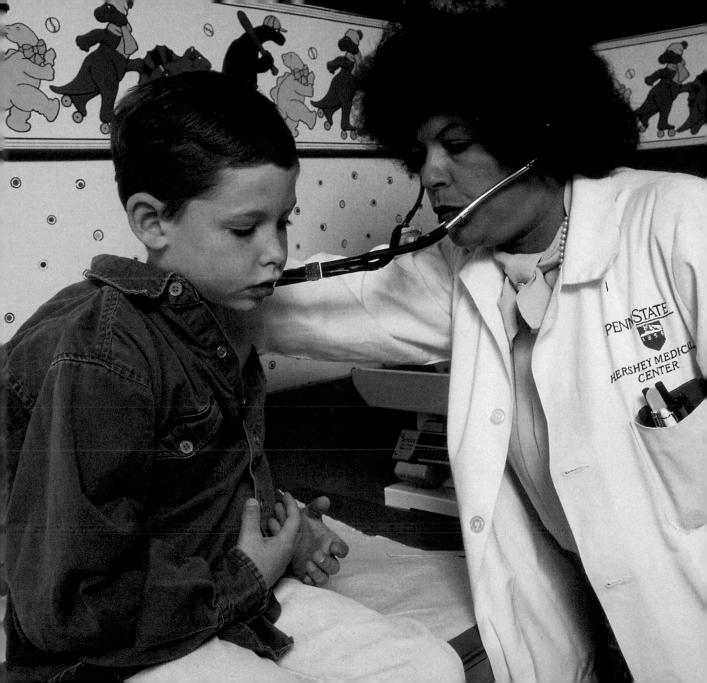

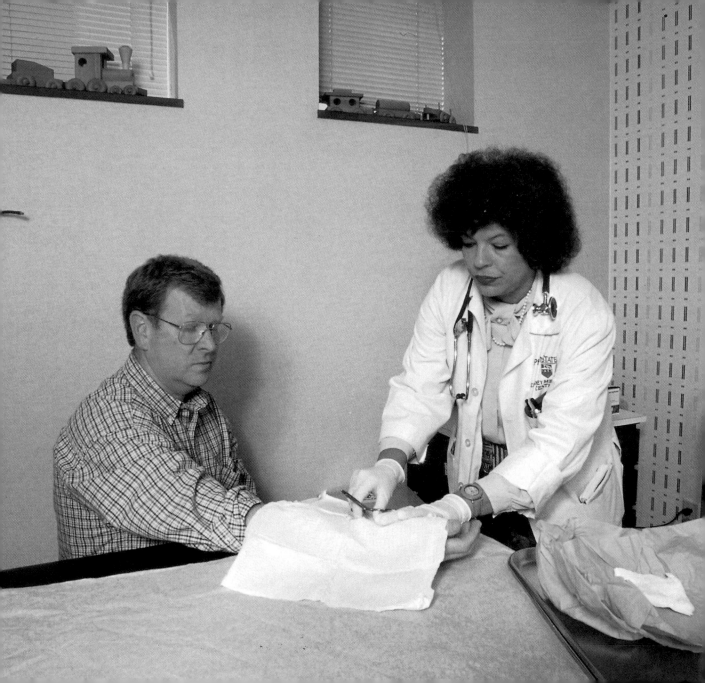

More Patients

Dr. Miller's next patient is a man. He has a cut on his arm.

Dr. Miller cleans the cut and sews it up with **stitches** (STIH-chcz).

"Keep your arm clean and dry so the cut can get better," she tells him. "We'll take the stitches out in a few days."

There are many patients waiting. Dr. Miller examines each one. She writes down on each chart what she does and what the patient should do to get better.

◀ Stitches are often used for cuts that are very deep.

Zöe Needs a Shot

Zöe has come to the office for a shot.

"I don't want a shot," says Zöe.

"I know, but you need one. It will keep you from getting sick," says Dr. Miller. "New medicines are being made every day. Soon you won't need shots anymore."

"But I'm scared," says Zöe.

"You don't have to be scared."

"Ouch!" says Zöe.

"It's all over," says Dr. Miller.

"That was quick. I guess I didn't have to be scared after all," says Zöe, smiling.

A shot only stings for a second, and then it is over. ▶

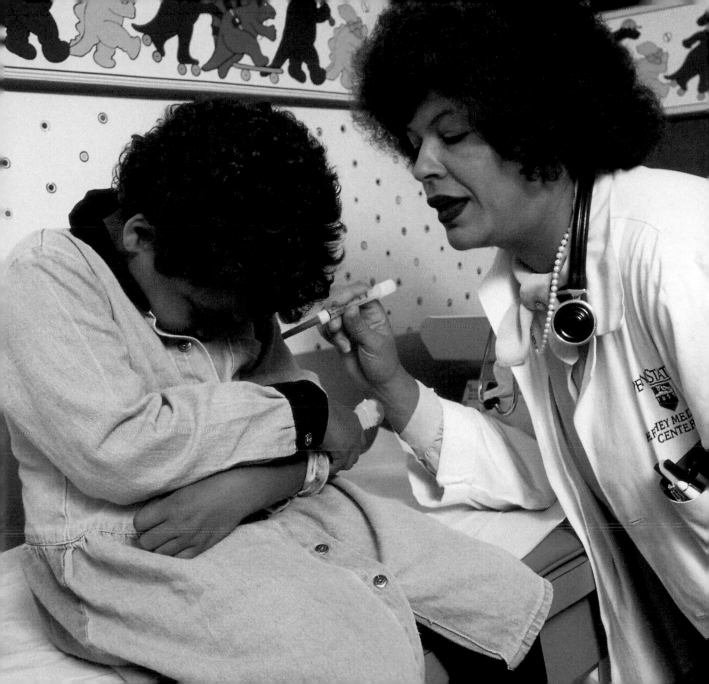

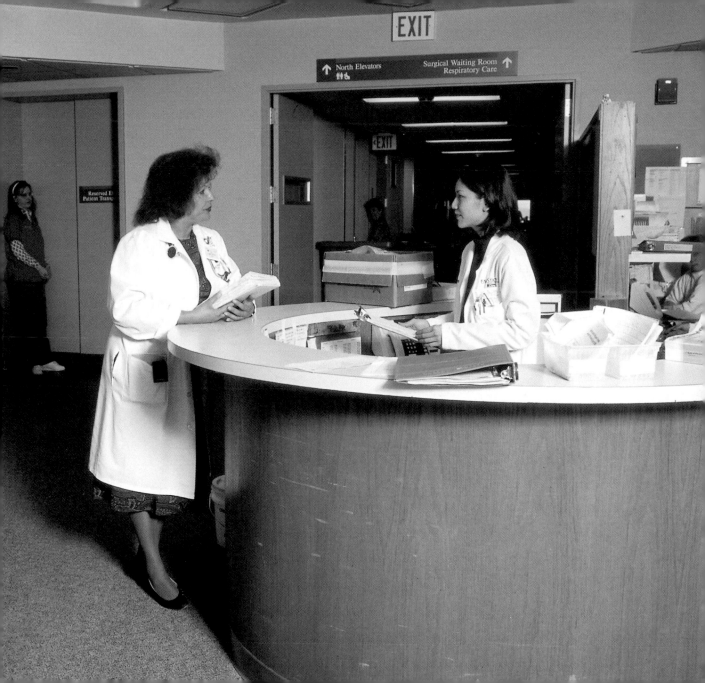

To the Hospital

After Dr. Miller sees her last patient in her office, she heads over to the **hospital** (HOS-pih-tul) to visit her patients there.

The patients are glad to see her. She examines them. She also checks their charts.

Most of the patients ask, "When can I go home?" The nurses take good care of them, but the patients want to go home as soon as Dr. Miller says they can.

"You can go home as soon as you are well," says Dr. Miller.

Dr. Miller checks her patients' charts to make sure they are getting the right medicines.

17

A Bad Bruise

Next Dr. Miller goes into one of the examining rooms to meet a new patient.

"I fell and hit my head this morning. And I still have a very bad headache," the patient says.

Dr. Miller looks at the patient's chart. She also looks at the **X rays** (EX-rayz) on the wall.

"Your X rays show that you are fine. But you have a bad bruise on your head," Dr. Miller says. "Get some rest. I will give you some medicine for your headache."

Sometimes Dr. Miller uses X rays to help her learn more about how a patient is hurt. ▶

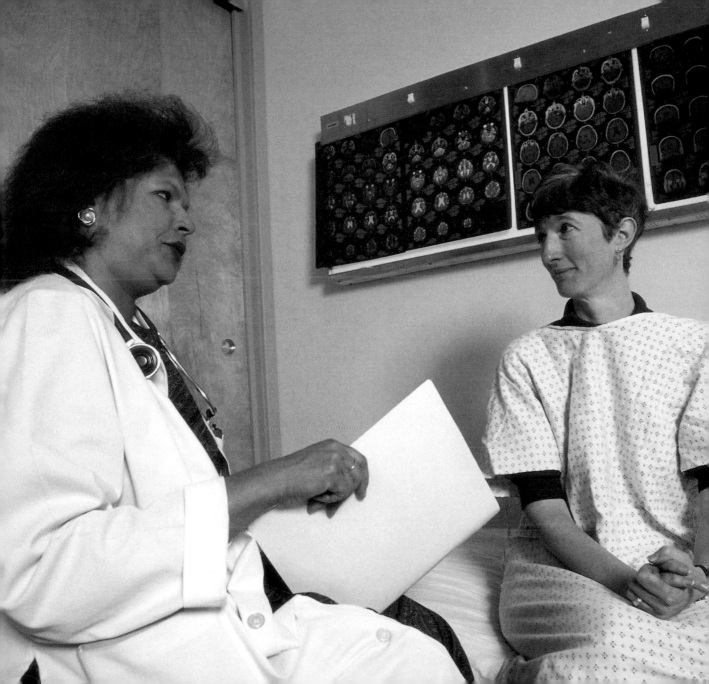

On Call

By 6:00 p.m., Dr. Miller has seen all of her patients in the hospital. But Dr. Miller is on call tonight. Before she gets home, her car phone rings. A patient needs her right away. Dr. Miller turns her car around and heads back to the hospital.

When doctors are on call, they are always ready to help patients in an **emergency** (ee-MER-jen-see). Doctors take turns being on call on different days.

◀ Being on call means always being ready to help patients who need a doctor.

Home at Last

When Dr. Miller gets home, her daughter, Lena, is already in bed. While Dr. Miller eats dinner, she reads about a new medicine. Doctors must keep studying so they can always do their best.

Tomorrow, another doctor will be on call. Then Dr. Miller and Lena can spend time together. Dr. Miller likes being a doctor. But she also likes being with her daughter. Being a doctor is a tough job, but that's okay for Dr. Miller. She likes to help people.

Glossary

emergency (ee-MER-jen-see) A sudden need for quick action.

examine (egg-ZAM-in) To look at something carefully.

germ (JERM) Tiny living things that can cause sickness.

hospital (HOS-pih-tul) A place for the care of the sick or hurt.

infected (in-FEK-ted) When something has been made sick by germs.

otoscope (AH-tuh-skohp) A tool used by a doctor to look into somebody's ears.

patient (PAY-shunt) Someone who goes to a doctor because he or she is sick or hurt.

stethoscope (STETH-uh-skohp) A tool doctors use to hear someone's heartbeat and lungs.

stitches (STIH-chez) Special thread used to close up a cut on somebody's body.

virus (VY-rus) A type of germ that can make a person sick.

X ray (EX-ray) A picture of part of the inside of your body.

Index